Design: David Kilpatrick

Layout: Kate Shanks

ISBN:

978-0-9962058-3-2 (print)

978-0-9962058-4-9 (digital)

Published by Beadle Books

New York

95 Theses on the Reformation of Football

Out of love and zeal for beauty and the desire to bring it to light, the following theses will be publicly discussed in New York at Mercy College under the professorship of David Kilpatrick, Doctor of Philosophy, Professor of English and Sport Management and regularly appointed lecturer on these subjects at that place. He requests that those who cannot be present to debate orally with us will do so by letter.

1.

Life must be justified, given meaning.

2.

Beauty justifies life.

3.

Work preserves but cannot justify life.

4.

We find meaning in play.

5.

Meaningful modes of play produce the sacred.

6.

The hieratic event stages myth, making meaning.

7.

Sport is a meaningful mode of play.

8.

The stadium has replaced the cathedral as the locus of spiritual life.

9.

Football is the most meaningful game.

10.

Association football is the beautiful game.

11.

Association football is the global game.

12.

Association football
is the superior code of
football.

13.

Care for the association code requires understanding its history and governance.

14.

Care for the association code requires understanding other codes of football.

15.

An essential element of the association code is associativity.

16.

Dissociative elements have threatened the association code since inception.

17.

The essence of team sport is associativity.

18.

Associativity is ultimately cosmopolitan.

19.

Olympism is the noble pursuit of sport's essence.

20.

Modern Olympism is flawed with its principle of sporting equity.

21.

Unlike men, all sports are not created equal.

22.

Modern football is a product of modernism and its antidote.

23.

Often innovation in football design is technological, beginning with trains and vulcanized rubber.

24.

Nonetheless, the simplicity of the association code is essential to its universality and superiority.

25.

The Laws of the Game, although not set in stone, must not be tampered with lightly.

26.

The Laws of the Game must not be pedantically asserted over trifles, disrupting the flow of play.

27.

The governance of the game must not compromise the Laws or essence of the game.

28.

The study of the Laws of the Game must not be restricted to referee education, but free and available to all who love the game.

29.

The game is best played in ideal weather conditions, cultivating environmental sensitivity.

30.

Internationalism
compromises
Olympism, which is
(like associativity)
essentially
cosmopolitan.

31.

The sacred may be rendered profane, subjected to the cynicism of utility and spoiled of its meaningful essence.

32.

Sport provides the most culturally meaningful events in modernity.

33.

Individual sports are most meritocratic while team sports are the most democratic, but most vulnerable to unfairness.

34.

Soccer's global prominence is an inevitable consequence of the prelusory goals at its essence, that make it the greatest of sports.

35.

The willful refusal of utility is the essence of the sacred.

36.

We work with our hands so playing with our feet — denying the equipmentality of the hands — is to transcend utility.

37.

Like a cheat who would handle the ball, there are those who seek to get their hands on the game with cynical utility.

38.

The sacred has been profaned and requires reformation.

39.

The delicate balance between technique and brutality makes the association code superior to other sports.

40.

The delicate balance between predictability and the prospect of upset makes the association code superior to other sports.

41.

The delicate balance
between attention and
endurance makes
the association code
superior to other
sports.

42.

The delicate balance
between individualism
and collectivism makes
the association code
superior to other
sports.

43.

The delicate balance between reason and passion makes the association code superior to other sports.

44.

The delicate balance between nature and technology makes the association code superior to other sports.

45.

The delicate balance and connectivity between local and global competitions makes the association code superior to other sports.

46.

Temporal and spatial standards of play preserve a universal alignment with this delicate balance for the most meaningful games.

47.

Annual and quadrennial competitions align play with natural, cosmic cycles.

48.

The disruption of
the most meaningful
games' alignment
with these cycles for
crass commercialism
threatens the game's
sacred power to provide
meaning.

49.

Care for the game requires attention to local and global levels of play.

50.

Corruption is found at local, regional, national, and international levels of the game's governance.

51.

Care for the game requires rooting out corruption at all levels.

52.

We need more meaningful games.

53.

More meaningful games are a matter of quality not quantity.

54.

Corruption in the game threatens to render it meaningless.

55.

The right to play is sacrosanct.

56.

Pay-to-play violates the right to play.

57.

Pay-to-play schemes deprive talent opportunities to develop and thrive.

58.

The deprivation of talent is the deprivation of beauty.

59.

The deprivation of beauty threatens to render the game meaningless.

60.

Inclusivity and opportunity must be afforded all who would play, at all ages and all levels of play.

61.

Elite sport should be meritocratic but now financial resources too often determine who plays.

62.

The simplicity of the association code should prevent its play from ever being considered a luxury for the privileged few.

63.

The beautiful game
(like rock music) is
fundamentally working
class if not culturally
classless.

64.

If the game can only be played and watched by the wealthy, abandoning its working-class roots, it will become culturally irrelevant, meaningless.

65.

Mediated views of the game cannot overcome the phenomenology of live drama anymore than cinema can surpass live theatre for performers and audiences alike.

66.

If the masses cannot play, they will not watch, they will not care, and the game's sacred role in society will be lost forever.

67.

The sole reason soccer remains culturally irrelevant in America is exclusivity.

68.

Whereas this exclusivity was once ethnic, it is now economic, despite preserved hegemony of a now geriatric oligarchy.

69.

Term limits for leadership positions not only prevent corruption with governance, they ensure fresh ideas and diverse perspectives.

70.

Lovers of the beautiful game in America are disenfranchised from the game's governance and grow ever more disillusioned.

71.

Franchise scarcity is a plight on the landscape of American sport.

72.

The adoption of the North American league sport model for association football leaves the game culturally marginal.

73.

Artificial franchise scarcity is antithetical to the essence of the association code, rooted in fraternal connectivity and inclusion.

74.

Cultivating empathy, the humanities must play a greater role in coaching and management education, player development, and sport criticism.

75.

Commerce should serve sport, not sport serving commerce, for commercialism exploits sacred play and spoils sport to profanity.

76.

We need a Temple cleansing to overcome the corruption and ineptitude of soccer's Sanhedrin.

77.

A global Super League could be culturally transformative, so long as it is rooted in an inclusive model with sporting integrity.

78.

A European Super League formed on the American franchise model with artificial scarcity threatens to render the game culturally irrelevant, meaningless.

79.

Conversely, the adoption of an associative, inclusive league model for soccer in North America would prove culturally transformative.

80.

Soccer cannot become the preeminent sport in the United States without the adoption of promotion and relegation and the dissolution of the single-entity league.

81.

The growth of the game cannot be hindered indefinitely by the interests of capital.

82.

While technology allowed for the game's birth and growth, it might well bring its death, lost as screened simulacra.

83.

VAR is the most blatant intrusion of commercial interests in the game, despite ethical pretensions.

84.

VAR is an aesthetic failure.

85.

VAR is an epistemic failure.

86.

VAR is no more than a Trojan horse to allow for commercial interruptions, disturbing the delicate balance of temporal limits.

87.

Gender equity is both the greatest promise of the game and its greatest opportunity for growth.

88.

The game will only find its full meaning when the women's game means as much as the men's game, regardless of nation.

89.

For 150 years, international play has been the most meaningful, but globalization will require club play to transcend national interests.

90.

A new model of global sporting governance must emerge to allow the game to enhance its sacred role for the future.

91.

As square and compass design the space of play, we must ensure the game through time achieves true universality in cosmodernity.

92.

Away then with all those cynical pundits who say to lovers of the beautiful game, "This is just business, the way of the world," for we make our world!

93.

Blessed be all those prophets of a better day for the beautiful game, that we may play with an ever-greater sense and depth of meaning.

94.

Lovers of the beautiful game should be exhorted to be diligent in pursuit of reform for the game, through scorn and derision.

95.

And thus be confident that through their efforts they bring light to darkness and let beauty flourish with the game.

Acknowledgements

The author would like to express his gratitude towards Nicholas Alexandrakos, Zachary Bigalke, Tom McCabe, Tyler Pittman, and Yunus Tuncel for feedback, Kate Shanks for layout, and especially Lisa, Dylan, and Honor Kilpatrick for their love and support.

David Kilpatrick is Professor of English and Sport Management at Mercy College, New York.

CPSIA information can be obtained
at www.ICGtesting.com
Printed in the USA
BVHW032129251122
652777BV00016B/1073

9 780996 205832